BABY'S BOOK

THE FIRST FIVE YEARS

PETER PAUPER PRESS, INC.
WHITE PLAINS, NEW YORK

PETER PAUPER PRESS
Fine Books and Gifts Since 1928

OUR COMPANY

In 1928, at the age of twenty-two, Peter Beilenson began printing books on a small press in the basement of his parents' home in Larchmont, New York. Peter—and later, his wife, Edna—sought to create fine books that sold at "prices even a pauper could afford."

Today, still family owned and operated, Peter Pauper Press continues to honor our founders' legacy—and our customers' expectations—of beauty, quality, and value.

Illustrations by Paper & Cloth

Text by Virginia Reynolds

Design by Heather Zschock

Copyright © 2017
Peter Pauper Press, Inc.
202 Mamaroneck Avenue
White Plains, NY 10601 USA
ISBN 978-1-4413-2484-9
Printed in China
7 6 5 4 3 2

Visit us at www.peterpauper.com

CONTENTS

GREAT EXPECTATIONS

A NEW BABY IS LIKE THE BEGINNING OF ALL THINGS —
WONDER, HOPE, A DREAM OF POSSIBILITIES.

EDA J. LESHAN

Place ultrasound picture or photo
of parents-to-be here.

When we found out we were expecting..

....

....

What we did to celebrate..

....

....

....

The people we told first...

....

....

Notes from pregnancy and preparations, including first hearing Baby's heartbeat, first feeling Baby move, and preparing for the grand arrival

....

....

....

....

SHOWERED WITH WELL WISHES

Our baby shower was given by...

It was held on .... at ....

The people who attended included:

Guest	*Gift*

SHOWER PHOTOS, MEMENTOS, AND MEMORIES

Place invitation and photos
from the shower here.

OUR GROWING FAMILY

Place family photos here.

BABY'S FAMILY TREE

Great-grandmother

_____
Name

_____
Birth date & place

Great-grandmother

_____
Name

_____
Birth date & place

Great-grandfather

_____
Name

_____
Birth date & place

Great-grandfather

_____
Name

_____
Birth date & place

Great-grandmother

_____
Name

_____
Birth date & place

Great-grandmother

_____
Name

_____
Birth date & place

Great-grandfather

_____
Name

_____
Birth date & place

Great-grandfather

_____
Name

_____
Birth date & place

Maternal grandmother

_____
Name

_____
Birth date & place

Paternal grandmother

_____
Name

_____
Birth date & place

Maternal grandfather

_____
Name

_____
Birth date & place

Paternal grandfather

_____
Name

_____
Birth date & place

Mother

_____
Name

_____
Birth date & place

Father

_____
Name

_____
Birth date & place

Baby!

_____
Name

ABOUT BABY'S MOTHER

Mother's full name..

Where Mother grew up..

Where Mother went to school..

Mother's interests, hobbies, and occupation..

....

....

Grandmother's name and some details about her...

....

....

Grandfather's name and some details about him...

....

....

Aunts and uncles on Mother's side...

....

....

A little bit about Mother's family history...

....

....

....

....

ABOUT BABY'S FATHER

Father's full name..

Where Father grew up...

Where Father went to school...

Father's interests, hobbies, and occupation...

....

....

Grandmother's name and some details about her...

....

....

Grandfather's name and some details about him..

....

....

Aunts and uncles on Father's side...

....

....

A little bit about Father's family history..

....

....

....

....

ABOUT BABY'S SIBLINGS

Sibling's name ....

When and where Sibling was born ....

A little bit about Sibling ....

Sibling's name ....

When and where Sibling was born ....

A little bit about Sibling ....

Sibling's name ....

When and where Sibling was born ....

A little bit about Sibling ....

Sibling's name ....

When and where Sibling was born ....

A little bit about Sibling ....

How Siblings feel about Baby's arrival ....

Place photo of siblings here.

WELCOME
TO THE WORLD!

A BABY IS BORN WITH A NEED TO BE LOVED —
AND NEVER OUTGROWS IT.

FRANK A. CLARK

Place newborn photo here.

BABY'S ARRIVAL!

Baby's full name..

The story behind Baby's name..

Nicknames...

The other names we considered ....

Baby was due on...

Baby was born on..

Time and place of birth...

Baby was delivered by...

The people who helped included ....

Baby came out:　　　Headfirst ☐　　　Feetfirst ☐　　　Via Caesarean ☐

Baby's weight.......................... Baby's length........................... Head circumference...........................

Hair color.............................. Eye color................................. Blood type ....

Birth tests and results...

....

The people in the room to greet Baby were...

....

Baby was especially cute because...

....

OUR THOUGHTS ON BABY'S BIRTH

Baby's birth story, from beginning to happy ending

Place photo of newborn and family here.

BABY'S MEMENTOS

Baby's tiny handprint and footprint

Baby's hospital bracelet

BIRTH ANNOUNCEMENT

Place announcement here.

WHAT THE WORLD WAS LIKE

NEWS HEADLINES ON THE DAY BABY WAS BORN

Place news clippings here.

Our notes about the world when Baby was born, including major news events; our country's leader; popular songs, books, and movies; the cost of things; and more.

....

....

....

....

....

....

COMING HOME

Baby's first address was...

....

Family members, friends, and pets waiting to welcome Baby...

....

....

How Baby's room looked..

....

....

Place photo here.

BABY'S FIRST DAYS AT HOME

How Baby slept...

....

Baby's personality..

....

....

Baby's feeding habits...

....

....

What was challenging...

....

....

What was amazing...

....

....

Special moments...

....

....

....

People who helped us care for Baby ....

....

....

The best advice we received ....

....

....

In those days, Baby was: a handful ☐   quiet and calm ☐

Thoughts about Baby's temperament ....

....

....

....

Our wishes, hopes, and dreams for Baby ....

....

....

....

....

....

Place photo here.

THE PEOPLE WHO VISITED BABY

(AND THE GIFTS THEY GAVE)

Name	Gift

CELEBRATING BABY'S ARRIVAL

BABY'S SPECIAL EVENT WAS...

a christening ☐   a bris ☐   a naming ceremony ☐   something else _____ ☐

It happened on _____ and was held at _____

The people who attended included _____

_____

_____

_____

Our thoughts and memories _____

_____

_____

_____

_____

_____

_____

*Place photos and other mementos
of the event here.*

ALL ABOUT BABY

EVERY CHILD BEGINS THE WORLD AGAIN.

HENRY DAVID THOREAU

Place photo here.

BABY'S HEALTH

Pediatrician's name .... Baby's first visit ....

Health notes ....

....

HOW BABY GREW!

AGE	WEIGHT	HEIGHT	NOTES
Birth			
Hospital discharge			
One month			
Two months			
Three months			
Four months			
Five months			
Six months			
Seven months			
Eight months			
Nine months			
Ten months			
Eleven months			
One year			
Fifteen months			
Eighteen months			
Twenty-one months			
Two years			
Two and one-half years			
Three years			
Three and one-half years			
Four years			
Four and one-half years			
Five years			

SAY CHEESE!

Baby began teething at .... weeks

Baby's first tooth appeared at .... months

How Baby fared with teething ....

Teething remedies ....

WHEN BABY'S TEETH APPEARED
(Write dates on tooth images.)

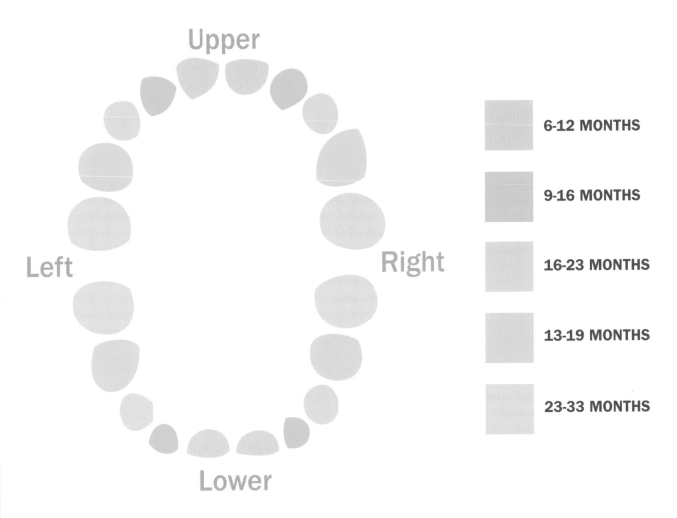

Upper

Left

Right

Lower

6-12 MONTHS

9-16 MONTHS

16-23 MONTHS

13-19 MONTHS

23-33 MONTHS

IMMUNIZATION RECORD
(TO AGE 5)

Parents: Check with Baby's doctor or nurse to ensure that your baby receives immunizations on time. Doctors' schedules may vary. Be sure to ask for a record card listing the dates of all immunizations. Bring the card to every visit.

VACCINE	DATE GIVEN	NOTES
Hepatitis B		
HepB (1)		
HepB (2)		
HepB (3)		
Rotavirus		
RV (1)		
RV (2)		
RV (3)		
Diphtheria, tetanus, pertussis		
DTaP (1)		
DTaP (2)		
DTaP (3)		
DTaP (4)		
DTaP (5)		
Haemophilus influenzae type b		
Hib (1)		
Hib (2)		
Hib (3)		
Hib (4)		

VACCINE	DATE GIVEN	NOTES
Pneumococcal		
PCV (1)		
PCV (2)		
PCV (3)		
PCV (4)		
Polio		
IPV (1)		
IPV (2)		
IPV (3)		
IPV (4)		
Measles, mumps, rubella		
MMR (1)		
MMR (2)		
Varicella		
Varicella (1)		
Varicella (2)		
Hepatitis A		
HepA (1)		
HepA (2)		
Influenza (yearly)		
Influenza		
Influenza		
Influenza		
Influenza		
Influenza		
Other		
Other		

BABY'S EATING HABITS

Baby stopped night feeding at .... weeks

Baby ate from a spoon at .... months

Baby drank from a cup at .... months

Baby began to eat independently at .... months

Baby's first solid food was ....

Baby: ☐ liked it ☐ hated it

The foods Baby liked best were ....

....

Notes about Baby's eating habits ....

....

....

Place photo here.

BABY'S SLEEPING HABITS

Baby slept through the night at .... months

Baby's bedtime rituals ....

....

Baby's best-loved blanket or comfort object ....

....

Lullabies Baby likes ....

....

Bedtime stories Baby prefers ....

....

Notes about Baby's sleeping habits ....

....

Place photo here.

BABY'S
FIRST YEAR

EVERY CHILD IS BORN A GENIUS.

R. BUCKMINSTER FULLER

Place photo here.

BABY'S MILESTONES

MILESTONE	DATE
Baby's first smile	
Baby's first laugh	
Baby's first sounds	
Baby held head up	
Slept through the night	
Rolled over	
Sat up	
Crawled	
Stood with support	
Stood alone	
Walked with help	
Walked alone	
Baby's first haircut	
Baby's first words	
More of baby's firsts and highlights	

BABY'S FIRST MONTH

What Baby could do ....

....

Baby's personality ....

....

What was challenging ....

....

What was amazing ....

....

Baby's likes and dislikes ....

....

Baby's eating habits ....

....

Baby's sleeping pattern and bedtime ritual ....

....

Special moments ....

....

....

....

Place photos here.

BABY'S SECOND MONTH

What Baby could do...

....

Baby's personality..

....

What was challenging..

....

What was amazing...

....

Baby's likes and dislikes...

....

Baby's eating habits..

....

Baby's sleeping pattern and bedtime ritual...

....

Special moments...

....

....

....

Place photos here.

BABY'S THIRD MONTH

What Baby could do...

....

Baby's personality...

....

What was challenging...

....

What was amazing..

....

Baby's likes and dislikes...

....

Baby's eating habits...

....

Baby's sleeping pattern and bedtime ritual...

....

Special moments..

....

....

Place photos here.

BABY'S FOURTH MONTH

What Baby could do..

....

Baby's personality...

....

What was challenging...

....

What was amazing...

....

Baby's likes and dislikes..

....

Baby's eating habits..

....

Baby's sleeping pattern and bedtime ritual...

....

Special moments..

....

....

Place photos here.

BABY'S FIFTH MONTH

What Baby could do..

....

Baby's personality..

....

What was challenging..

....

What was amazing..

....

Baby's likes and dislikes..

....

Baby's eating habits..

....

Baby's sleeping pattern and bedtime ritual..

....

Special moments..

....

....

....

Place photos here.

BABY'S SIXTH MONTH

What Baby could do..

....

Baby's personality..

....

What was challenging..

....

What was amazing..

....

Baby's likes and dislikes...

....

Baby's eating habits..

....

Baby's sleeping pattern and bedtime ritual...

....

Special moments...

....

....

....

Place photos here.

BABY'S SEVENTH MONTH

What Baby could do...

....

Baby's personality...

....

What was challenging...

....

What was amazing..

....

Baby's likes and dislikes..

....

Baby's eating habits..

....

Baby's sleeping pattern and bedtime ritual...

....

Special moments..

....

....

....

Place photos here.

BABY'S EIGHTH MONTH

What Baby could do...

....

Baby's personality...

....

What was challenging...

....

What was amazing...

....

Baby's likes and dislikes..

....

Baby's eating habits..

....

Baby's sleeping pattern and bedtime ritual...

....

Special moments...

....

....

....

Place photos here.

BABY'S NINTH MONTH

What Baby could do...

....

Baby's personality...

....

What was challenging...

....

What was amazing...

....

Baby's likes and dislikes..

....

Baby's eating habits..

....

Baby's sleeping pattern and bedtime ritual..

....

Special moments..

....

....

....

Place photos here.

BABY'S TENTH MONTH

What Baby could do..

....

Baby's personality...

....

What was challenging..

....

What was amazing..

....

Baby's likes and dislikes...

....

Baby's eating habits..

....

Baby's sleeping pattern and bedtime ritual..

....

Special moments...

....

....

....

Place photos here.

BABY'S ELEVENTH MONTH

What Baby could do ....

....

Baby's personality ....

....

What was challenging ....

....

What was amazing ....

....

Baby's likes and dislikes ....

....

Baby's eating habits ....

....

Baby's sleeping pattern and bedtime ritual ....

....

Special moments ....

....

....

....

Place photos here.

BABY'S TWELFTH MONTH

What Baby could do..

....

Baby's personality..

....

What was challenging...

....

What was amazing...

....

Baby's likes and dislikes...

....

Baby's eating habits..

....

Baby's sleeping pattern and bedtime ritual..

....

Special moments..

....

....

....

Place photos here.

ONE TO TWO YEARS OLD

ONE IS FUN!

KIDS ARE FASCINATED BY STORIES ABOUT WHAT
THEY WERE LIKE WHEN THEY WERE BABIES AND
WHAT THEY SAID AND DID AS THEY GREW.

STEPHANIE MARSTON

Photos and mementos from Baby's first birthday party

BABY'S FIRST BIRTHDAY PARTY

Date, time, and place..

How we celebrated...

....

....

Who was there...

....

....

Gifts Baby received...

....

....

What Baby thought of all the festivities...

....

....

Memorable moments...

....

....

BABY'S MILESTONES AND ACHIEVEMENTS

MILESTONE	DATE
Baby's first scribbles	
First imitated the behavior of others	
Pointed to objects when asked	
Began stacking blocks	
Picked up toys	
Played with push/pull toys	
Danced	
Used own name	
Turned pages one by one	
Removed clothing without help	
Walked up and down stairs while holding onto a rail	
Pointed to pictures in a book	
Followed simple directions	
First friends and playmates	
Baby's other milestones and highlights	

Reminder to parents: All children develop at their own pace. The ages for these milestones are approximate and don't necessarily reflect the development of every child.

NOTES AND PHOTOS

ALL ABOUT BABY

The foods Baby likes best..

Favorite activities..

....

Favorite toys...

Stories and songs Baby likes best..

....

Baby's special places...

....

Things Baby doesn't like..

....

Baby's finest adventure...

....

That cute thing Baby says or does..

....

The best way to make Baby laugh..

....

Baby's personality...

....

LOOK WHO'S TALKING

Sounds Baby likes to make..

....

New words...

....

Baby's first sentence..

....

SOCIAL SKILLS AND ACTIVITIES

Baby's preferred caregivers...

....

Baby's playmates and friends...

....

Where Baby went to daycare/nursery school..

....

Baby's teachers...

Things we did together...

....

....

NOTES AND PHOTOS

NOTES AND PHOTOS

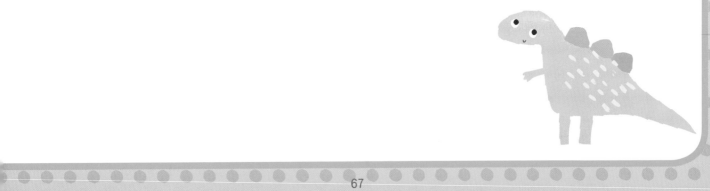

TWO TO THREE
YEARS OLD

WHOO-HOO! BABY'S TWO.

WHEN WE PARTICIPATE IN THE GROWTH OF CHILDREN,
A SENSE OF WONDER MUST TAKE HOLD OF US,
PROVIDING FOR US A SENSE OF THE FUTURE.

GRETA HOFMANN NEMIROFF

Photos and mementos from Baby's second birthday party

BABY'S SECOND BIRTHDAY PARTY

Date, time, and place ....

How we celebrated ....

....

....

Who was there ....

....

....

Gifts Baby received ....

....

....

What Baby thought of all the festivities ....

....

....

Memorable moments ....

....

....

BABY'S MILESTONES AND ACHIEVEMENTS

MILESTONE	DATE
Used simple sentences	
Could name the parts of their body	
Could follow simple directions	
Used pronouns correctly	
Named toys	
Began to pretend	
Played with a ball	
Used a spoon correctly	
Used negative sentences	
Could wash and dry hands	
Started watching children play	
Started joining in	
Baby's other milestones and highlights	

Reminder to parents: All children develop at their own pace. The ages for these milestones are approximate and don't necessarily reflect the development of every child.

NOTES AND PHOTOS

ALL ABOUT BABY

The foods Baby likes best..

Favorite activities..

....

Favorite toys..

Stories and songs Baby likes best..

....

Baby's special places..

....

Things Baby doesn't like...

....

Baby's finest adventure...

....

That cute thing Baby says or does...

....

The best way to make Baby laugh..

....

Baby's personality..

....

....

NOTES AND PHOTOS

SOCIAL SKILLS AND ACTIVITIES

Baby's preferred caregivers

Baby's playmates and friends

Where Baby went to daycare/nursery school

Baby's teachers

Cute sayings

Things we did together

NOTES AND PHOTOS

THREE TO FOUR YEARS OLD

WHEE! BABY'S THREE.

GROWN-UPS NEVER UNDERSTAND ANYTHING FOR THEMSELVES, AND IT IS TIRESOME FOR CHILDREN TO BE ALWAYS AND FOREVER EXPLAINING THINGS TO THEM.

-ANTOINE DE SAINT-EXUPÉRY, *THE LITTLE PRINCE*

Photos and mementos from Baby's third birthday party

BABY'S THIRD BIRTHDAY PARTY

Date, time, and place ....

How we celebrated ....

....

....

Who was there ....

....

....

Gifts Baby received ....

....

....

....

What Baby thought of all the festivities ....

....

....

....

Memorable moments ....

....

....

....

BABY'S MILESTONES AND ACHIEVEMENTS

MILESTONE	DATE
Started showing a variety of emotions	
Brushed teeth unassisted	
Understood and obeyed (or not!) simple rules	
Talked about things that happened in the past	
Started using blunt scissors	
Used a swing alone	
Understood taking turns	
Baby's other milestones and highlights	

Reminder to parents: All children develop at their own pace. The ages for these milestones are approximate and don't necessarily reflect the development of every child.

NOTES AND PHOTOS

ALL ABOUT BABY

The foods Baby likes best

Favorite activities

Favorite toys

Stories and songs Baby likes best

Baby's special places

Things Baby doesn't like

Baby's finest adventure

That cute thing Baby says or does

The best way to make Baby laugh

Baby's personality

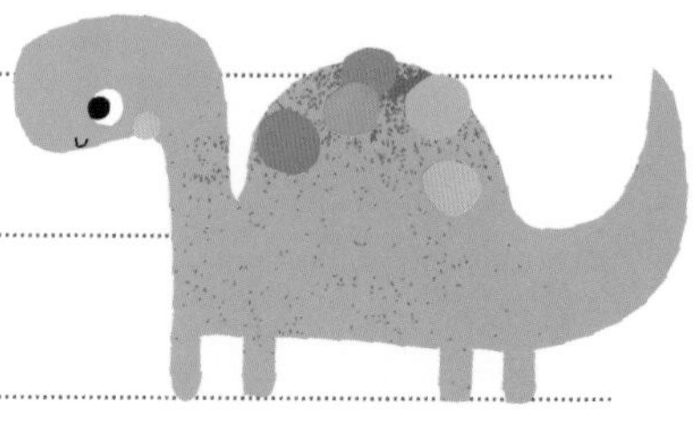

NOTES AND PHOTOS

SOCIAL SKILLS AND ACTIVITIES

Baby's preferred caregivers...

....

Baby's playmates and friends..

....

....

Where Baby went to daycare/nursery school..

....

Baby's teachers...

....

....

Cute sayings..

....

....

Things we did together...

....

....

....

NOTES AND PHOTOS

IMAGINATION AND CREATIVITY

Ways Baby likes to express self

....

....

....

Things Baby likes to draw

....

....

....

Craft projects we do together

....

....

....

Songs Baby likes

....

....

....

Baby's musical abilities

....

....

NOTES AND PHOTOS

NOTES AND PHOTOS

NOTES AND PHOTOS

FOUR TO FIVE YEARS OLD

READY TO ROAR – BABY'S FOUR!

THERE ARE NO SEVEN WONDERS OF THE WORLD IN THE EYES OF A CHILD. THERE ARE SEVEN MILLION.

WALT STREIGHTIFF

Photos and mementos from Baby's fourth birthday party

BABY'S FOURTH BIRTHDAY PARTY

Date, time, and place...

How we celebrated...

....

Who was there...

....

....

....

Gifts Baby received...

....

....

....

What Baby thought of all the festivities..

....

Memorable moments...

....

....

....

....

BABY'S MILESTONES AND ACHIEVEMENTS

MILESTONE	DATE
Told a simple story or related an event	
Skipped	
Tied shoes	
Asked how, why, and when questions	
Could recite own street and town	
Could string small beads	
Could catch a ball easily	
Baby's other milestones and highlights	

Reminder to parents: All children develop at their own pace. The ages for these milestones are approximate and don't necessarily reflect the development of every child.

NOTES AND PHOTOS

ALL ABOUT BABY

The best thing about being four ....

....

What Baby wants to be when grown up ....

The foods Baby likes best are ....

Favorite activities ....

....

Toys Baby is fond of ....

Stories and songs Baby likes best ....

Repeated rhymes and songs Baby likes ....

Baby's special places ....

....

Things Baby doesn't like ....

Baby's finest adventure ....

....

That cute thing Baby says or does ....

The best way to make Baby laugh ....

Baby's personality ....

....

NOTES AND PHOTOS

SOCIAL SKILLS AND ACTIVITIES

Baby's preferred caregivers..

....

....

Baby's playmates and friends..

....

....

....

Cute sayings..

....

....

....

Things we did together..

....

....

....

....

NOTES AND PHOTOS

FIRST HANDWRITING

Baby's autograph here   Date

....

....

Have Baby write and/or draw something here.

....

....

....

NOTES AND PHOTOS

BEYOND FIVE YEARS OLD

DIVE INTO FIVE!

ALL I REALLY NEED TO KNOW ABOUT HOW TO LIVE AND WHAT
TO DO AND HOW TO BE I LEARNED IN KINDERGARTEN.

ROBERT FULGHUM

Photos and mementos from Baby's fifth birthday party

BABY'S FIFTH BIRTHDAY PARTY

Date, time, and place...

....

How we celebrated...

....

Who was there...

....

Gifts Baby received..

....

What Baby thought of all the festivities..

....

Memorable moments..

....

....

....

....

....

ALL ABOUT KINDERGARTEN

Things we looked forward to..

....

Things we worried about..

....

Where Baby went to school...

....

First day of kindergarten..

....

Baby's teacher was..

....

Baby's new friends and classmates..

....

Activities Baby enjoys..

....

Our memories of Baby's first day...

....

....

....

NOTES AND PHOTOS

SPECIAL DAYS

CHILDREN WILL NOT REMEMBER YOU FOR
THE MATERIAL THINGS YOU HAVE PROVIDED BUT FOR
THE FEELING THAT YOU CHERISHED THEM.

RICHARD L. EVANS

Place photos and mementos here.

FAMILY GATHERINGS

OCCASION .... DATE

Where it took place ....

....

People who shared the event with us ....

....

....

Our memories of the occasion ....

....

....

....

*Place photos and
mementos here.*

FAMILY GATHERINGS

OCCASION _____ DATE _____

Where it took place...

People who shared the event with us...

....

....

Our memories of the occasion...

....

....

....

*Place photos and
mementos here.*

HOLIDAYS

HOLIDAY .... DATE

Where we spent the holiday ....

People who shared the holiday with us ....

....

Our special holiday memories ....

....

....

....

....

Place photos and
mementos here.

HOLIDAYS

HOLIDAY _____   DATE _____

Where we spent the holiday ....

People who shared the holiday with us ....

....

Our special holiday memories ....

....

....

....

*Place photos and
mementos here.*

HOLIDAYS

HOLIDAY .... DATE _____

Where we spent the holiday ....

People who shared the holiday with us ....

....

Our special holiday memories ....

....

....

*Place photos and
mementos here.*

VACATIONS AND TRIPS

WHERE WE WENT _____ DATE _____

What we did ....

Our memories of the trip ....

....

....

....

....

Place photos and
mementos here.

VACATIONS AND TRIPS

WHERE WE WENT _____ DATE _____

What we did..

Our memories of the trip...

....

....

....

....

Place photos and mementos here.

VACATIONS AND TRIPS

WHERE WE WENT .... DATE

What we did ....

Our memories of the trip ....

....

....

....

....

....

Place photos and mementos here.

NOTES AND PHOTOS

DEAR BABY

Our wishes, hopes, and dreams for Baby